Easy Home Cooking

Holiday COOKIES

PUBLICATIONS INTERNATIONAL, LTD.

Easy Home Cooking is a trademark of Publications International, Ltd.

Photography: Sanders Studio, Inc.
Photographer: Kathy Sanders
Photo Assistant: Cristin Nestor
Food Stylists: Donna Coates, Gail O'Donnell, Carol Parik
Assistant Food Stylist: Kim Hartman
Prop Stylist: Patty Higgins
Studio Coordinator: Kathy Ores

Pictured on the front cover: Almond Crescents *(page 58)*, Cappuccino Cookies *(page 90)*, Chocolate Caramel Nut Bars *(page 34)*, Cocoa Crinkle Sandwiches *(page 70)*, Fruitcake Slices *(page 84)*, Gingerbread People *(page 76)*, Holiday Sugar Cookies *(page 64)*, Raspberry Pecan Thumbprints *(page 66)* and Special Treat No-Bake Squares *(page 42)*.

Pictured on the back cover *(clockwise from top left):* Molded Scotch Shortbread *(page 68)*, Chocolate Chip Brownies *(page 54)* and Holiday Sugar Cookies *(page 64)*.

ISBN: 0-7853-2615-4

Manufactured in U.S.A.

8 7 6 5 4 3 2 1

Nutritional Analysis: In the case of multiple choices, the first ingredient, the lowest amount and the lowest serving yield are used to calculate the nutritional analysis. "Serve with" suggestions are not included unless otherwise stated. Serving size in this publication is one piece.

Easy Home Cooking™

Holiday Cookies

p. 84

The Basics

What better way to celebrate the holidays than with homemade cookies? Always popular, cookies are perfect for every occasion, from small family gatherings to big neighborhood parties, plus they make great gifts. And best of all, so many cookies are so easy to make—you won't want to wait for the holidays to start baking!

The seemingly endless variety of cookies can be divided into several basic types: drop, bar, refrigerator, shaped and rolled. These types are determined by the consistency of the dough and how it is formed into cookies.

DROP COOKIES

Drop cookies are as quick and easy as their name suggests: simply mix the batter as directed and drop it by the spoonful onto a baking sheet. Use one spoon to scoop up the batter and another to push it off, spacing the cookies about 2 inches apart. Try to make them all about the same size and shape so they finish baking at the same time.

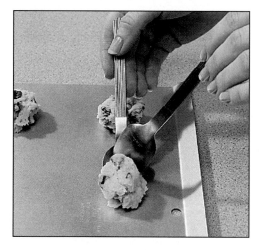

BAR COOKIES

Also a snap to make, bar cookies only require preparing the batter and spreading it in a pan. For best results, be sure to use the pan size called for in the recipe, otherwise the texture will be affected. Grease the pan only if the recipe tells you to do so—some cookies don't need it. Once they have cooled, bar cookies can be cut into squares or rectangles, or try triangles, irregular chunks or bite-size bits for variety.

REFRIGERATOR COOKIES

Refrigerator cookie dough is shaped into a log and chilled until firm before slicing and baking. After shaping the dough, wrap the log securely in waxed paper or plastic wrap so that air will not dry out the dough, then refrigerate until firm. (The wrapped dough can be stored several days in the refrigerator and even longer in the freezer, offering great make-ahead convenience for the busy holiday season.)

When firm, slice the dough with a sharp knife and a gentle back-and-forth sawing motion, rotating the log occasionally to keep one side from flattening.

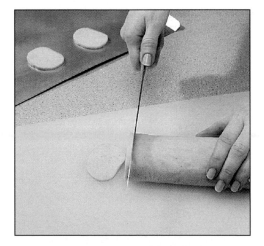

For decorated edges, roll the log in a variety of coatings. Or, leave them plain and decorate after baking.

SHAPED COOKIES

This cookie dough is easily formed into balls, logs or crescents with your hands.

The cookies can then be decorated before baking: rolled in sugar, filled with jam, topped with candies or flattened with a fork. Or decorate them after baking.

This collection of shaped cookies also includes cookies that are cut out into shapes. This dough must be chilled first, then rolled out on a floured surface with a floured rolling pin. (Keep all remaining dough wrapped in the refrigerator while you work so it does not dry out.) For the best results, dip the edge of your cookie cutter in flour and press down firmly to cut out the dough. Using a rolling pin cover and pastry cloth can make rolling out the dough easier—these tools minimize dough-sticking problems and prevent too much flour absorbing into the dough and making it tough.

COOKIE BAKING DONENESS CHART

Cookie type	Doneness test
drop cookies	lightly browned and slight imprint remains after touching surface with fingertip
fudgey bar cookies	surface appears dull and slight imprint remains after touching surface with fingertip
cakey bar cookies	wooden toothpick inserted in center comes out clean
refrigerator cookies	edges are firm and bottoms are lightly browned
shaped cookies	edges are lightly browned
rolled cookies	edges are firm and bottoms are lightly browned

MEASURE UP!

Measure accurately! Cookie recipes require exact measurements to turn out right.

- Dry measuring cups come in nested sets. For flour and powdered sugar, stir them first, spoon into the proper measuring cup and then level off the top with the straight edge of a knife. For brown sugar, pack firmly into a dry measuring cup before leveling off.

- Measuring spoons also come in sets; ingredients other than liquids should also be leveled off with the straight edge of a knife.

- Liquid measuring cups come in several sizes with amounts marked on the side of the cups. Place the cup on a flat surface, pour in the liquid to be measured and then read the measurement at eye level.

- Don't measure any ingredients directly over your mixing bowl, as they could easily spill over and ruin the recipe.

GENERAL GUIDELINES

- Read the entire recipe before you begin—make sure you have everything you need.

- Remove butter, margarine and cream cheese from the refrigerator to soften, if necessary.

- Toast and chop nuts, peel and slice fruit and melt chocolate before preparing the dough.

- Grease cookie sheets *only* when the recipe recommends it, otherwise the cookies may spread too much.

- Always preheat the oven about 10 minutes before baking.

- When baking more than one sheet of cookies at a time, rotate them from top to bottom halfway through the baking time.

- Check cookies for doneness at the minimum baking time given in each recipe.

EASY DECORATING IDEAS

Chocolate for dipping or drizzling

Place 1 cup of chocolate chips in a small microwavable bowl; microwave on High 1 to 1½ minutes, stirring after 1 minute. Stir until smooth. Dip the cookies and place on waxed paper until the chocolate is set. (You can dip the whole cookie, half, or just the edges.) For quick drizzling, simply use a spoon or fork to drizzle chocolate over the cookies.

For more artistic drizzling (patterns or writing), melt the chocolate chips in a small resealable plastic freezer bag. Cut off a very tiny corner of the bag and squeeze out the chocolate to form designs.

Powdered sugar glaze or icing

Cookies such as oatmeal, spice or molasses look and taste great with a non-chocolate topping. Use the recipes on page 24 and 28 any time you want to dip or drizzle cookies with an easy white glaze.

Powdered sugar

The quickest and easiest of toppings—just a dusting of powdered sugar adds a beautiful finishing touch to many cookies and bars.

Nuts

Whole, halved, chopped and sliced nuts can add extra flavor and crunch to cookies and bars.

Colored sugar, sprinkles and candies

The possibilities are endless—and easy! Simply sprinkle on top and bake!

Prepared toppings

Bottled ice cream toppings, such as fudge, caramel or butterscotch can be used for a quick decorative drizzle over cookies and bars.

GIFT–GIVING TIPS

Storage

• Store soft and crisp cookies separately at room temperature to prevent changes in texture and color.

• Keep soft cookies in airtight containers to retain moisture; keep crisp cookies in containers with loose-fitting lids to prevent moisture buildup.

• Store cookies with sticky glazes, fragile decorations and icings in single layers between sheets of waxed paper.

Packing

• Soft, moist cookies can survive packing and shipping better than fragile, brittle cookies.

• Brownies and bar cookies generally pack well, but avoid those with moist fillings and frostings since they tend to become sticky at room temperature.

• Wrap each type of cookie separately to retain flavors and textures. Pack wrapped cookies in rows as tightly as possible to prevent breakage during shipping.

Containers

Choose from the containers below and add your own personal touch along with the cookies: a cloth napkin, tissue paper, ribbons or raffia. You might also include your recipes, hand written on decorative cards.

Baskets: Available in a wide variety of sizes, shapes and colors, baskets can be easily decorated with colored tissue or cellophane wrap and ribbon.

Airtight canisters and tins: Also found in many different sizes and colors, these containers hold up well during shipping.

Assorted pails: Plastic and metal pails make inexpensive and fun cookie containers, especially for children's gifts.

Gift bags and boxes: Craft and party stores sell a wide variety of decorative bags and boxes perfect for any cookie-giving occasion.

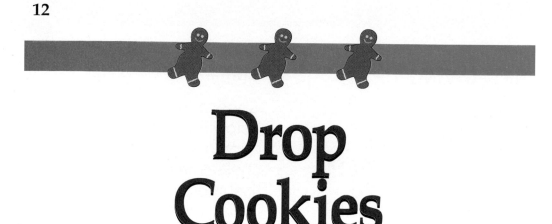

Drop Cookies

Toffee Chunk Brownie Cookies

1 cup butter
4 ounces unsweetened
    chocolate, coarsely
    chopped
1½ cups sugar
2 eggs

1 tablespoon vanilla
3 cups all-purpose flour
⅛ teaspoon salt
1½ cups coarsely chopped
    chocolate-covered
    toffee bars

PREHEAT oven to 350°F. Melt butter and chocolate in large saucepan over low heat, stirring until smooth. Remove from heat; cool slightly.

STIR sugar into chocolate mixture until smooth. Stir in eggs until well blended. Stir in vanilla until smooth. Stir in flour and salt just until mixed. Fold in chopped toffee.

DROP heaping tablespoonfuls of dough 1½ inches apart onto *ungreased* cookie sheets.

BAKE 12 minutes or until just set. Let cookies stand on cookie sheets 5 minutes; transfer to wire racks to cool completely. Store in airtight container.   *Makes 36 cookies*

Nutrients per Serving: Calories: 171, Total Fat: 8 g, Protein: 2 g, Carbohydrate: 23 g, Cholesterol: 28 mg, Sodium: 61 mg, Dietary Fiber: 1 g Dietary Exchanges: 1½ Bread, 1½ Fat

Peanut Gems

2½ cups all-purpose flour
1 teaspoon baking powder
⅛ teaspoon salt
1 cup butter, softened
1 cup packed light brown
   sugar

2 eggs
2 teaspoons vanilla
1½ cups cocktail peanuts,
   finely chopped
Powdered sugar
   (optional)

PREHEAT oven to 350°F. Combine flour, baking powder and salt in small bowl.

BEAT butter in large bowl with electric mixer at medium speed until smooth. Gradually beat in brown sugar; increase speed to medium-high and beat until light and fluffy. Beat in eggs, 1 at a time, until fluffy. Beat in vanilla. Gradually stir in flour mixture until blended. Stir in peanuts until blended.

DROP heaping tablespoonfuls of dough about 1 inch apart onto *ungreased* cookie sheets; flatten slightly with hands.

BAKE 12 minutes or until set. Let cookies stand on cookie sheets 5 minutes; transfer to wire racks to cool completely. Dust cookies with powdered sugar, if desired. Store in airtight container.

Makes 30 cookies

Nutrients per Serving: Calories: 172, Total Fat: 11 g, Protein: 3 g, Carbohydrate: 17 g, Cholesterol: 32 mg, Sodium: 96 mg, Dietary Fiber: 1 g
Dietary Exchanges: 1 Bread, 2 Fat

Cook's Nook

Peanuts can be chopped quickly and easily in the food processor. Use brief on/off pulses, taking care not to overprocess (or you'll end up with peanut butter).

Ultimate Chippers

2½ cups all-purpose flour
1 teaspoon baking soda
½ teaspoon salt
1 cup butter or margarine, softened
1 cup packed light brown sugar
½ cup granulated sugar

2 eggs
1 tablespoon vanilla
1 cup vanilla chips
1 cup semisweet chocolate chips
1 cup milk chocolate chips
½ cup coarsely chopped pecans (optional)

PREHEAT oven to 375°F. Combine flour, baking soda and salt in medium bowl.

BEAT butter, brown sugar and granulated sugar in large bowl with electric mixer at medium speed until light and fluffy. Beat in eggs and vanilla. Add flour mixture; beat at low speed just until blended. Stir in chips and pecans.

DROP heaping teaspoonfuls of dough 2 inches apart onto *ungreased* cookie sheets.*

BAKE 10 to 12 minutes or until edges are golden brown. Let cookies stand on cookie sheets 2 minutes; transfer to wire racks to cool completely. Store tightly covered at room temperature or freeze up to 3 months.   *Makes about 72 cookies*

*Or, use a small ice cream scoop (#90) filled with dough and pressed against the side of the bowl to level.

Nutrients per Serving: Calories: 94, Total Fat: 5 g, Protein: 1 g, Carbohydrate: 12 g, Cholesterol: 14 mg, Sodium: 67 mg, Dietary Fiber: trace
Dietary Exchanges: ½ Bread, 1 Fat

Maple Walnut Meringues

⅓ cup powdered sugar
½ cup plus ⅓ cup ground
    walnuts, divided
¾ cup packed light brown
    sugar

3 egg whites, at room
    temperature
Pinch salt
⅛ teaspoon cream of tartar
1 teaspoon maple extract

PLACE 1 oven rack in top third of oven and 1 oven rack in bottom third of oven; preheat oven to 300°F. Line 2 large cookie sheets with aluminum foil, shiny side up.

STIR powdered sugar and ½ cup walnuts with fork in medium bowl; set aside. Crumble brown sugar into small bowl; set aside.

BEAT egg whites and salt in large bowl with electric mixer at high speed until foamy. Add cream of tartar; beat 30 seconds or until mixture forms soft peaks. Sprinkle brown sugar, 1 tablespoon at a time, over egg white mixture; beat at high speed until each addition is completely absorbed. Beat 2 to 3 minutes or until mixture forms stiff peaks. Beat in maple extract at low speed. Fold in walnut mixture with large rubber spatula.

DROP level tablespoonfuls of dough to form mounds about 1 inch apart on prepared cookie sheets. Sprinkle cookies with remaining ⅓ cup ground walnuts. Bake 25 minutes or until cookies feel dry on surface but remain soft inside. (Rotate cookie sheets from top to bottom halfway through baking time.)

SLIDE foil with cookies onto wire racks; cool completely. Carefully remove cookies from foil. Store in airtight container with waxed paper between layers of cookies. Cookies are best the day they are baked.

Makes about 36 cookies

Nutrients per Serving: Calories: 41, Total Fat: 2 g, Protein: 1 g, Carbohydrate: 6 g, Cholesterol: 0 mg, Sodium: 6 mg, Dietary Fiber: trace
Dietary Exchanges: 2½ Bread, ½ Fat

Buttery Almond Cookies

1¼ cups all-purpose flour
½ teaspoon baking powder
⅛ teaspoon salt
1¼ cups slivered almonds,
    divided

10 tablespoons butter,
    softened
¾ cup sugar
1 egg
1 teaspoon vanilla

PREHEAT oven to 350°F. Grease cookie sheets. Combine flour, baking powder and salt in small bowl.

FINELY CHOP ¾ cup almonds; set aside.

BEAT butter in large bowl with electric mixer at medium speed until smooth. Gradually beat in sugar until blended; increase speed to high and beat until light and fluffy. Beat in egg until fluffy. Beat in vanilla until blended. Stir in flour mixture until blended. Stir in chopped almonds just until combined.

DROP rounded teaspoonfuls of dough about 2 inches apart onto prepared cookie sheets. Top each cookie with several slivered almonds, pressing into dough.

BAKE 12 minutes or until edges are golden brown. Let cookies stand on cookie sheets 5 minutes; transfer to wire racks to cool completely. Store in airtight container.   *Makes about 42 cookies*

Nutrients per Serving: Calories: 75, Total Fat: 5 g, Protein: 1 g, Carbohydrate: 7 g, Cholesterol: 13 mg, Sodium: 13 mg, Dietary Fiber: trace
Dietary Exchanges: ½ Bread, 1 Fat

Chocolate Chip Macaroons

2½ cups flaked coconut
⅔ cup mini semisweet
chocolate chips

⅔ cup sweetened
condensed milk
1 teaspoon vanilla

PREHEAT oven to 350°F. Grease cookie sheets; set aside.

COMBINE coconut, chips, milk and vanilla in medium bowl; stir until well blended.

DROP rounded teaspoonfuls of dough 2 inches apart onto prepared cookie sheets. Press dough gently with back of spoon to flatten slightly.

BAKE 10 to 12 minutes or until light golden brown. Let cookies stand on cookie sheets 1 minute; transfer to wire racks to cool completely. Store tightly covered at room temperature. (These cookies do not freeze well.)   *Makes about 42 cookies*

Nutrients per Serving: Calories: 49, Total Fat: 3 g, Protein: 1 g, Carbohydrate: 6 g, Cholesterol: 2 mg, Sodium: 7 mg, Dietary Fiber: trace
Dietary Exchanges: ½ Bread, ½ Fat

Store unopened cans of sweetened condensed milk at room temperature up to 6 months. Store any leftover milk in an airtight container up to 5 days.

Oatmeal Raisin Cookies

¾ cup all-purpose flour
¾ teaspoon salt
½ teaspoon baking soda
½ teaspoon ground cinnamon
¾ cup butter or margarine, softened
¾ cup granulated sugar
¾ cup packed light brown sugar

1 egg
1 tablespoon water
1 tablespoon vanilla, divided
3 cups uncooked quick or old-fashioned oats
1 cup raisins
½ cup powdered sugar
1 tablespoon milk

PREHEAT oven to 375°F. Grease cookie sheets; set aside. Combine flour, salt, baking soda and cinnamon in small bowl.

BEAT butter, granulated sugar and brown sugar in large bowl with electric mixer at medium speed until light and fluffy. Add egg, water and 2 teaspoons vanilla; beat well. Add flour mixture; beat at low speed just until blended. Stir in oats with spoon. Stir in raisins.

DROP tablespoonfuls of dough 2 inches apart onto prepared cookie sheets.

BAKE 10 to 11 minutes or until edges are golden brown. Let cookies stand 2 minutes on cookie sheets; transfer to wire racks to cool completely.

For glaze: **STIR** powdered sugar, milk and remaining 1 teaspoon vanilla in small bowl until smooth. Drizzle over cookies with fork or spoon. Store cookies tightly covered at room temperature or freeze up to 3 months.   *Makes about 48 cookies*

Nutrients per Serving: Calories: 93, Total Fat: 3 g, Protein: 1 g, Carbohydrate: 15 g, Cholesterol: 12 mg, Sodium: 79 mg, Dietary Fiber: trace Dietary Exchanges: 1 Bread, ½ Fat

Nutty Clusters

4 squares (1 ounce each) unsweetened chocolate, divided
1 cup granulated sugar
½ cup plus 2 tablespoons butter or margarine, softened, divided
1 egg

⅓ cup buttermilk
1 teaspoon vanilla
1¾ cups all-purpose flour
½ teaspoon baking soda
1 cup mixed salted nuts, coarsely chopped
2 cups powdered sugar
2 to 3 tablespoons water

For cookies: **PREHEAT** oven to 400°F. Line cookie sheets with parchment paper or leave ungreased. Melt 2 squares chocolate in heavy small saucepan over very low heat. Remove from heat; let cool.

BEAT granulated sugar and ½ cup butter in large bowl with electric mixer until smooth. Beat in melted chocolate, egg, buttermilk and vanilla until light. Stir in flour and baking soda just until blended. Stir in nuts.

DROP teaspoonfuls of dough 2 inches apart onto prepared cookie sheets.

BAKE 8 to 10 minutes or until almost no imprint remains when touched. Immediately transfer cookies to wire rack.

Meanwhile, for icing, **MELT** remaining 2 squares chocolate and 2 tablespoons butter in small heavy saucepan over low heat, stirring until completely melted. Add powdered sugar and water, mixing until smooth. Frost cookies while still warm.   *Makes about 48 cookies*

Nutrients per Serving: *Calories: 106, Total Fat: 5g, Protein: 1 g, Carbohydrate: 14 g, Cholesterol: 11 mg, Sodium: 62 mg, Dietary Fiber: trace Dietary Exchanges: 1 Bread, 1 Fat*

Soft Molasses Spice Cookies

2¼ cups all-purpose flour
1 teaspoon baking soda
1 teaspoon ground
   cinnamon
½ teaspoon ground ginger
¼ teaspoon ground nutmeg
⅛ teaspoon salt
⅛ teaspoon ground cloves
½ cup plus 2 tablespoons
   butter, softened,
   divided

½ cup packed dark brown
   sugar
1 egg
½ cup molasses
1¼ teaspoons vanilla,
   divided
¼ cup plus 2 to
   3 tablespoons
   milk, divided
¾ cup raisins (optional)
2 cups powdered sugar

PREHEAT oven to 350°F. Grease cookie sheets. Combine flour, baking soda, cinnamon, ginger, nutmeg, salt and cloves in medium bowl.

BEAT ½ cup butter in large bowl with electric mixer at medium speed until smooth and creamy. Gradually beat in brown sugar until blended; increase speed to high and beat until light and fluffy. Beat in egg until fluffy. Beat in molasses and 1 teaspoon vanilla until smooth. Beat in flour mixture at low speed alternately with ¼ cup milk until blended. Stir in raisins.

DROP rounded tablespoonfuls of dough about 1½ inches apart onto prepared cookie sheets. Bake 12 minutes or until set. Let cookies stand on cookie sheets 5 minutes; transfer to wire racks to cool completely.

For icing: **MELT** remaining 2 tablespoons butter in small saucepan over medium-low heat. Remove from heat; add powdered sugar and stir until blended. Add remaining 2 tablespoons milk and ¼ teaspoon vanilla; stir until smooth. If icing is too thick, add milk, 1 teaspoon at a time, until desired consistency.

SPREAD icing over tops of cookies. Let stand 15 minutes or until icing is set. Store in airtight container.   *Makes about 36 cookies*

Nutrients per Serving: Calories: 109, Total Fat: 4 g, Protein: 1 g,
Carbohydrate: 18 g, Cholesterol: 15 mg, Sodium: 65 mg, Dietary Fiber: trace
Dietary Exchanges: 1 Bread, ½ Fat

Cowboy Cookies

½ cup butter or margarine, softened

½ cup packed light brown sugar

¼ cup granulated sugar

1 egg

1 teaspoon vanilla

1 cup all-purpose flour

2 tablespoons unsweetened cocoa

½ teaspoon baking powder

¼ teaspoon baking soda

1 cup uncooked quick or old-fashioned oats

1 cup semisweet chocolate chips

½ cup raisins

½ cup chopped nuts

PREHEAT oven to 375°F. Lightly grease cookie sheets or line with parchment paper.

BEAT butter and sugars in large bowl with electric mixer until well blended. Add egg and vanilla; beat until fluffy.

COMBINE flour, cocoa, baking powder and baking soda in small bowl; stir into butter mixture with oats, chocolate chips, raisins and nuts.

DROP teaspoonfuls of dough 2 inches apart onto prepared cookie sheets.

BAKE 10 to 12 minutes or until lightly browned around edges. Transfer to wire racks to cool.   *Makes about 48 cookies*

Nutrients per Serving: Calories: 74, Total Fat: 4 g, Protein: 1 g, Carbohydrate: 10 g, Cholesterol: 10 mg, Sodium: 32 mg, Dietary Fiber: trace
Dietary Exchanges: ½ Bread, 1 Fat

Harvest Pumpkin Cookies

2 cups all-purpose flour
1 teaspoon baking powder
1 teaspoon ground
    cinnamon
½ teaspoon baking soda
½ teaspoon salt
½ teaspoon ground allspice
1 cup butter, softened

1 cup sugar
1 cup canned pumpkin
1 egg
1 teaspoon vanilla
1 cup chopped pecans
1 cup dried cranberries
    (optional)
Pecan halves (about 36)

PREHEAT oven to 375°F. Combine flour, baking powder, cinnamon, baking soda, salt and allspice in medium bowl.

BEAT butter and sugar in large bowl with electric mixer at medium speed until light and fluffy. Beat in pumpkin, egg and vanilla. Gradually add flour mixture. Beat at low speed until well blended. Stir in chopped pecans and cranberries with spoon.

DROP heaping tablespoonfuls of dough 2 inches apart onto *ungreased* cookie sheets. Flatten slightly with back of spoon. Press one pecan half into center of each cookie.

BAKE 10 to 12 minutes or until golden brown. Let cookies stand on cookie sheets 1 minute; transfer to wire racks to cool completely. Store tightly covered at room temperature or freeze up to 3 months.

Makes about 36 cookies

Note: If dried cranberries are not available, substitute raisins or currants.

Nutrients per Serving: Calories: 126, Total Fat: 8 g, Protein: 1 g, Carbohydrate: 12 g, Cholesterol: 20 mg, Sodium: 110 mg, Dietary Fiber: 1 g Dietary Exchanges: 1 Bread, 1½ Fat

Bar Cookies

Chocolate Caramel Nut Bars

1 package (18¼ ounces)
 devil's food cake mix
¾ cup butter or margarine,
 melted
½ cup milk, divided

60 vanilla caramels
1 cup cashew pieces,
 coarsely chopped
1 cup semisweet chocolate
 chips

PREHEAT oven to 350°F. Grease 13×9-inch baking pan. Combine cake mix, butter and ¼ cup milk in medium bowl; mix well. Press half of batter into bottom of prepared pan.

BAKE 7 to 8 minutes or until batter just begins to form crust. Remove from oven.

Meanwhile, **COMBINE** caramels and remaining ¼ cup milk in heavy medium saucepan. Cook over low heat, stirring often, about 5 minutes or until caramels are melted and mixture is smooth.

POUR melted caramel mixture over partially baked crust. Combine cashews and chocolate chips; sprinkle over caramel mixture.

DROP spoonfuls of remaining batter evenly over nut mixture. Return pan to oven; bake 18 to 20 minutes more or until top cake layer springs back when lightly touched. (Caramel center will be soft.) Cool on wire rack before cutting into squares or bars. (Bars can be frozen; let thaw 20 to 25 minutes before serving.)   *Makes about 48 bars*

Nutrients per Serving: Calories: 285, Total Fat: 16 g, Protein: 3 g, Carbohydrate: 38 g, Cholesterol: 16 mg, Sodium: 289 mg, Dietary Fiber: trace
Dietary Exchanges: 1½ Bread, 2½ Fat

Dish: **Bar Cookies**

Recipe
Serves:

Chocolate-Caramel-Nut Bars

1 package (18¼ ounces) devil's food cake mix
¾ cup butter or margarine, melted
½ cup milk, divided
60 vanilla caramels
1 cup cashew pieces, coarsely chopped
1 cup semisweet chocolate chips

PREHEAT oven to 350°F. Grease 13x9-inch ba
Combine cake mix, butter and ¼ cup milk in m

Luscious Lemon Bars

2 cups all-purpose flour
1 cup butter
½ cup powdered sugar
4 teaspoons grated lemon
    peel, divided

¼ teaspoon salt
1 cup granulated sugar
3 eggs
⅓ cup fresh lemon juice
    Sifted powdered sugar

PREHEAT oven to 350°F. Grease 13×9-inch baking pan.

COMBINE flour, butter, powdered sugar, 1 teaspoon lemon peel and salt in food processor. Process until mixture forms coarse crumbs. Press mixture evenly into prepared pan.

BAKE 18 to 20 minutes or until golden brown.

Meanwhile, **BEAT** remaining 3 teaspoons lemon peel, granulated sugar, eggs and lemon juice in medium bowl with electric mixer at medium speed until well blended.

POUR mixture evenly over warm crust. Return pan to oven; bake 18 to 20 minutes or until center is set and edges are golden brown. Cool completely on wire rack.

DUST with sifted powdered sugar; cut into bars. Store tightly covered at room temperature. (Do not freeze.)   *Makes 3 dozen bars*

Nutrients per Serving: Calories: 105, Total Fat: 6 g, Protein: 1 g, Carbohydrate: 13 g, Cholesterol: 31 mg, Sodium: 72 mg, Dietary Fiber: trace
Dietary Exchanges: 1 Bread, 1 Fat

You can squeeze more juice from lemons at room temperature than from refrigerated lemons.

Naomi's Revel Bars

1 cup plus 2 tablespoons
     butter or margarine,
     softened, divided
2 cups packed brown sugar
2 eggs
2 teaspoons vanilla
2½ cups all-purpose flour
1 teaspoon baking soda

3 cups uncooked quick or
     old-fashioned oats
1 package (12 ounces)
     semisweet chocolate
     chips
1 can (14 ounces)
     sweetened condensed
     milk

PREHEAT oven to 325°F. Lightly grease 13×9-inch baking pan.

BEAT 1 cup butter and sugar in large bowl with electric mixer until blended. Add eggs; beat until light. Blend in vanilla.

COMBINE flour and baking soda in medium bowl; stir into butter mixture. Stir in oats. Spread ¾ of oat mixture evenly in prepared pan.

COMBINE chocolate chips, milk and remaining 2 tablespoons butter in heavy small saucepan. Stir over low heat until chocolate is melted. Pour chocolate mixture evenly over oat mixture in pan. Dot with remaining oat mixture.

BAKE 20 to 25 minutes or until edges are browned and center feels firm. Cool on wire rack. Cut into bars.   *Makes about 36 bars*

Nutrients per Serving: Calories: 238, Total Fat: 10 g, Protein: 4 g, Carbohydrate: 35 g, Cholesterol: 31 mg, Sodium: 116 mg, Dietary Fiber: 1 g Dietary Exchanges: 2 Bread, 2 Fat

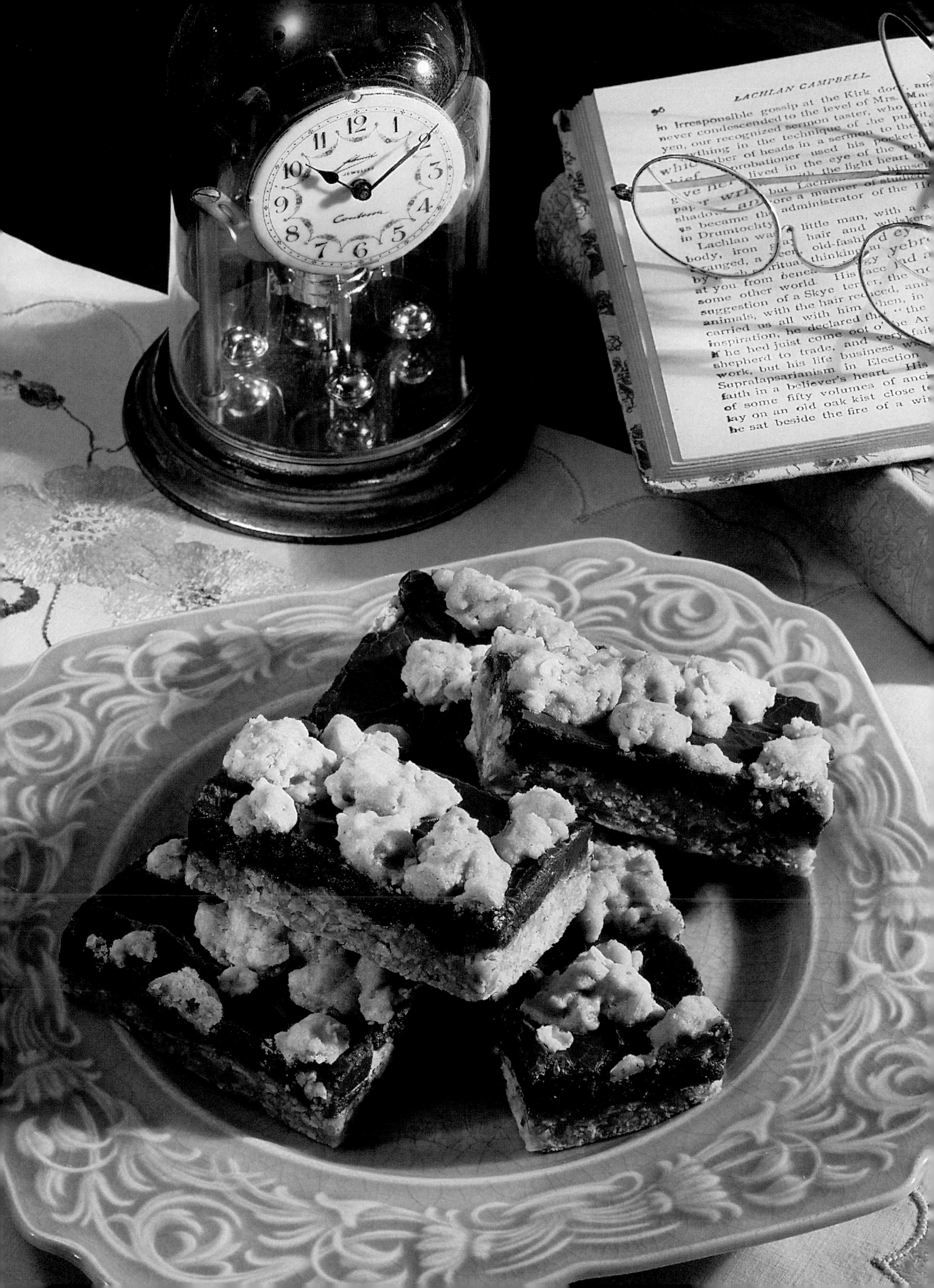
LACHLAN CAMPBELL

Yuletide Linzer Bars

1⅓ cups butter or margarine, softened

¾ cup sugar

1 egg

1 teaspoon grated lemon peel

2½ cups all-purpose flour

1½ cups whole almonds, ground

1 teaspoon ground cinnamon

¾ cup raspberry preserves

Powdered sugar

PREHEAT oven to 350°F. Grease 13×9-inch baking pan.

BEAT butter and sugar in large bowl with electric mixer until creamy. Beat in egg and lemon peel until blended. Mix in flour, almonds and cinnamon until well blended.

PRESS 2 cups dough into bottom of prepared pan. Spread preserves over crust. Press remaining dough, a small amount at a time, evenly over preserves.

BAKE 35 to 40 minutes until golden brown. Cool on wire rack. Sprinkle with powdered sugar; cut into bars.   *Makes 36 bars*

Nutrients per Serving: Calories: 160, Total Fat: 10 g, Protein: 2 g, Carbohydrate: 7 g, Cholesterol: 24 mg, Sodium: 72 mg, Dietary Fiber: trace Dietary Exchanges: 1 Bread, 2 Fat

Wetting your hands slightly before handling dough will prevent it from sticking to your hands.

Special Treat No-Bake Squares

½ cup plus ⅓ cup plus
    1 teaspoon butter or
    margarine, divided
¼ cup granulated sugar
¼ cup unsweetened cocoa
1 large egg
¼ teaspoon salt
1½ cups graham cracker
    crumbs (about
    18 graham crackers)

¾ cup flaked coconut
½ cup chopped pecans
1 package (3 ounces)
    cream cheese, softened
1 teaspoon vanilla
1 cup powdered sugar
2 ounces dark sweet or
    bittersweet chocolate
    candy bar, broken into
    ½-inch pieces

LINE 9-inch square pan with foil, shiny side up, allowing 2-inch overhang on sides. Or, lightly grease pan; set aside.

For crust: **COMBINE** ½ cup butter, granulated sugar, cocoa, egg and salt in medium saucepan. Cook over medium heat, stirring constantly, until mixture thickens, about 2 minutes. Remove from heat. Stir in graham cracker crumbs, coconut and pecans. Press evenly into prepared pan.

For filling: **BEAT** ⅓ cup butter, cream cheese and vanilla in small bowl with electric mixer at medium speed until smooth. Gradually beat in powdered sugar. Spread over crust; refrigerate 30 minutes.

For glaze: **COMBINE** candy bar and remaining 1 teaspoon butter in small resealable plastic food storage bag; seal bag. Microwave on HIGH 50 seconds. Turn bag over; microwave on HIGH 40 to 50 seconds or until melted. Knead bag until mixture is smooth.

CUT off very tiny corner of bag; drizzle chocolate over filling. Refrigerate until firm, about 20 minutes. Remove foil from pan. Cut into 1½-inch squares. Store tightly covered in refrigerator.

Makes 25 squares

Nutrients per Serving: *Calories: 166, Total Fat: 12 g, Protein: 2 g, Carbohydrate: 6 g, Cholesterol: 29 mg, Sodium: 137 mg, Dietary Fiber: trace Dietary Exchanges: 1 Bread, 2 Fat*

Strawberry Oat Bars

1 cup butter or margarine, softened
1 cup firmly packed light brown sugar
2 cups uncooked quick oats
1 cup all-purpose flour

2 teaspoons baking soda
½ teaspoon ground cinnamon
¼ teaspoon salt
1 can (21 ounces) strawberry pie filling
¾ teaspoon almond extract

PREHEAT oven to 375°F. Beat butter in large bowl with electric mixer at medium speed until smooth. Add sugar; beat until well blended.

COMBINE oats, flour, baking soda, cinnamon and salt in large bowl; mix well. Add flour mixture to butter mixture, beating on low speed until well blended and crumbly.

SPREAD ⅔ of crumb mixture in bottom of *ungreased* 13×9-inch baking pan, pressing down to form firm layer. Bake 15 minutes; let cool 5 minutes on wire rack

Meanwhile, **PLACE** strawberry filling in food processor or blender; process until smooth. Stir in almond extract.

POUR strawberry mixture over partially baked crust. Sprinkle remaining crumb mixture evenly over strawberry layer.

RETURN pan to oven; bake 20 to 25 minutes or until topping is golden brown and filling is slightly bubbly. Let cool completely on wire rack before cutting into bars.   *Makes about 48 bars*

Nutrients per Serving: Calories: 86, Total Fat: 4 g, Protein: 1 g, Carbohydrate: 12 g, Cholesterol: 10 mg, Sodium: 110 mg, Dietary Fiber: trace Dietary Exchanges: 2 Bread, 1½ Fat

Decadent Blonde Brownies

1 jar (3½ ounces) macadamia nuts
1½ cups all-purpose flour
1 teaspoon baking powder
½ teaspoon salt
¾ cup granulated sugar
¾ cup packed light brown sugar

½ cup butter or margarine, softened
2 eggs
2 teaspoons vanilla
1 package (10 ounces) semisweet chocolate chunks*

PREHEAT oven to 350°F. Generously grease 13×9-inch baking pan.

COARSELY chop enough macadamia nuts to measure ¾ cup. Combine flour, baking powder and salt in small bowl.

BEAT granulated sugar, brown sugar and butter in large bowl with electric mixer at medium speed until light and fluffy. Beat in eggs and vanilla. Add flour mixture; beat at low speed until well blended. Stir in macadamia nuts and chocolate chunks. Spread batter evenly in prepared pan.

BAKE 25 to 30 minutes or until golden brown. Cool completely on wire rack before cutting into bars. Store tightly covered at room temperature or freeze up to 3 months.   *Makes 24 brownies*

*If chocolate chunks are not available, cut 10-ounce thick chocolate candy bar into ½-inch pieces to equal 1½ cups.

Nutrients per Serving: Calories: 203, Total Fat: 11 g, Protein: 2 g, Carbohydrate: 27 g, Cholesterol: 28 mg, Sodium: 105 mg, Dietary Fiber: 1 g Dietary Exchanges: 2 Bread, 1½ Fat

Pecan Pie Bars

¾ cup butter or margarine
½ cup powdered sugar
1½ cups all-purpose flour
3 eggs
2 cups coarsely chopped
   pecans

1 cup granulated sugar
1 cup light corn syrup
2 tablespoons butter or
   margarine, melted
1 teaspoon vanilla

PREHEAT oven to 350°F.

For crust: **BEAT** ¾ cup butter in large bowl with electric mixer at medium speed until smooth. Add powdered sugar; beat until well blended.

ADD flour gradually, beating at low speed after each addition. (Mixture will be crumbly but presses together easily.)

PRESS dough evenly into *ungreased* 13×9-inch baking pan. Press mixture slightly up sides of pan (less than ¼ inch) to form lip to hold filling.

BAKE 20 to 25 minutes or until golden brown. Meanwhile, for filling, beat eggs lightly in medium bowl with fork. Add pecans, granulated sugar, corn syrup, melted butter and vanilla; mix well.

POUR filling over partially baked crust. Return to oven; bake 35 to 40 minutes or until filling is set.

LOOSEN edges with knife. Cool completely on wire rack before cutting into squares. Cover and refrigerate until 10 to 15 minutes before serving time. (Do not freeze.)   *Makes about 48 bars*

Nutrients per Serving: Calories: 119, Total Fat: 7 g, Protein: 1 g, Carbohydrate: 14 g, Cholesterol: 22 mg, Sodium: 43 mg, Dietary Fiber: trace Dietary Exchanges: 1 Bread, 1 Fat

No-Fuss Bar Cookies

24 graham cracker squares
1 cup semisweet chocolate
  chips
1 cup flaked coconut

¾ cup coarsely chopped
  walnuts
1 can (14 ounces)
  sweetened condensed
  milk

PREHEAT oven to 350°F. Grease 13×9-inch baking pan.

PLACE graham crackers in food processor. Process until crackers form fine crumbs. Measure 2 cups of crumbs.

COMBINE graham cracker crumbs, chips, coconut and walnuts in medium bowl; stir to blend. Add milk; stir until blended. Spread batter evenly in prepared pan.

BAKE 15 to 18 minutes or until edges are golden brown. Cool completely on wire rack before cutting. Cut into bars. Store tightly covered at room temperature or freeze up to 3 months.

Makes 20 bars

Nutrients per Serving: *Calories: 185, Total Fat: 9 g, Protein: 4 g, Carbohydrate: 25 g, Cholesterol: 7 mg, Sodium: 77 mg, Dietary Fiber: trace Dietary Exchanges: ½ Milk, 1 Bread, 1 Fat*

It's best to purchase nuts in small quantities, as their high fat content makes them go rancid more quickly than other dry ingredients. Store nuts in an airtight container in a cool, dry place.

Currant Cheesecake Bars

½ **cup butter or margarine, softened**
1 **cup all-purpose flour**
½ **cup packed light brown sugar**
½ **cup finely chopped pecans**
1 **package (8 ounces) cream cheese, softened**

¼ **cup granulated sugar**
1 **egg**
1 **tablespoon milk**
2 **teaspoons grated lemon peel**
⅓ **cup currant jelly or seedless raspberry jam**

PREHEAT oven to 350°F. Grease 9-inch square baking pan. Beat butter in medium bowl with electric mixer at medium speed until smooth. Add flour, brown sugar and pecans; beat at low speed until well blended. Press mixture into bottom and partially up sides of prepared pan.

BAKE about 15 minutes or until light brown. If sides of crust have shrunk down, press back up and reshape with spoon. Cool 5 minutes on wire rack.

Meanwhile, **BEAT** cream cheese in large bowl with electric mixer at medium speed until smooth. Add granulated sugar, egg, milk and lemon peel; beat until well blended.

HEAT jelly in small saucepan over low heat 2 to 3 minutes or until smooth, stirring occasionally.

POUR cream cheese mixture over crust. Drizzle jelly in 7 to 8 strips across filling with spoon. Swirl jelly through filling with knife to create marbled effect.

RETURN pan to oven; bake 20 to 25 minutes or until filling is set. Cool completely on wire rack before cutting into bars. Store in airtight container in refrigerator up to 1 week.   *Makes about 32 bars*

Nutrients per Serving: *Calories: 105, Total Fat: 7 g, Protein: 1 g, Carbohydrate: 11 g, Cholesterol: 22 mg, Sodium: 54 mg, Dietary Fiber: trace Dietary Exchanges: 1 Bread, 1 Fat*

Chocolate Chip Brownies

¾ cup granulated sugar
½ cup butter or margarine
2 tablespoons water
2 cups semisweet
  chocolate chips or mini
  chocolate chips,
  divided

1½ teaspoons vanilla
1¼ cups all-purpose flour
½ teaspoon baking soda
½ teaspoon salt
2 eggs
  Powdered sugar
  (optional)

PREHEAT oven to 350°F. Grease 9-inch square baking pan.

COMBINE granulated sugar, butter and water in medium microwavable mixing bowl. Microwave on HIGH 2½ to 3 minutes or until butter is melted. Stir in 1 cup chocolate chips; stir gently until chips are melted and mixture is well blended. Stir in vanilla; let stand 5 minutes to cool.

COMBINE flour, baking soda and salt in small bowl. Beat eggs, 1 at a time, into chocolate mixture. Add flour mixture; mix well. Stir in remaining 1 cup chocolate chips. Spread batter evenly in prepared pan.

BAKE 25 minutes for fudgy brownies or 30 to 35 minutes for cakelike brownies. Cool completely on wire rack. Cut into 2¼-inch squares. Place powdered sugar in fine-mesh strainer and sprinkle over brownies, if desired. Store tightly covered at room temperature or freeze up to 3 months. *Makes 16 brownies*

Nutrients per Serving: Calories: 236, Total Fat: 12 g, Protein: 3 g, Carbohydrate: 31 g, Cholesterol: 44 mg, Sodium: 182 mg, Dietary Fiber: trace Dietary Exchanges: 2 Bread, 2 Fat

Wait until cookies and bars have cooled completely before dusting them with powdered sugar—otherwise, the sugar will dissolve and disappear!

No-Bake Chocolate Oat Bars

1 cup butter or margarine
½ cup firmly packed brown
    sugar
1 teaspoon vanilla
3 cups uncooked
    quick oats

1 cup semisweet chocolate
    chips
½ cup crunchy or creamy
    peanut butter

GREASE 9-inch square baking pan. Melt butter in large saucepan over medium heat. Add sugar and vanilla; mix well.

STIR in oats. Cook over low heat 2 to 3 minutes or until ingredients are well blended. Press half of mixture into prepared pan. Use back of large spoon to spread mixture evenly.

Meanwhile, **MELT** chocolate chips in small heavy saucepan over low heat, stirring occasionally. Stir in peanut butter until smooth.

POUR chocolate mixture over oat mixture in pan; spread evenly with knife or back of spoon. Crumble remaining oat mixture over chocolate layer, pressing in gently. Cover and refrigerate 2 to 3 hours or overnight.

BRING to room temperature before cutting into bars. (Bars can be frozen; let thaw 10 minutes or more before serving.)

Makes 32 bars

Nutrients per Serving: Calories: 142, Total Fat: 10 g, Protein: 3 g, Carbohydrate: 13 g, Cholesterol: 15 mg, Sodium: 79 mg, Dietary Fiber: 1 g
Dietary Exchanges: 1 Bread, 1½ Fat

Shaped Cookies

Almond Crescents

· ·

1 cup plus 1 tablespoon butter or margarine, softened	**1 teaspoon vanilla**
⅓ cup granulated sugar	**1½ cups ground almonds, toasted***
1¾ cups all-purpose flour	**½ cup semisweet chocolate chips**
¼ cup cornstarch	

PREHEAT oven to 325°F. For crescents, beat 1 cup butter and granulated sugar in large bowl until creamy.

STIR in flour, cornstarch and vanilla. Stir in almonds. Shape tablespoonfuls of dough into crescents. Place 2 inches apart on *ungreased* cookie sheets.

BAKE 22 to 25 minutes or until light brown. Let cookies stand on cookie sheets 1 minute; transfer to wire racks to cool completely.

For glaze: **PLACE** chocolate chips and remaining 1 tablespoon butter in small resealable plastic food storage bag. Place bag in bowl of hot water 2 to 3 minutes until chocolate is softened. Knead until chocolate is smooth. Snip pinpoint corner in bag; drizzle chocolate over cookies. Allow chocolate to set before storing in airtight container.   *Makes about 36 cookies*

*To toast almonds, spread on cookie sheet. Bake at 325°F for 4 minutes or until fragrant and golden.

Variation: Instead of glaze, sprinkle crescents with powdered sugar before serving.

Nutrients per Serving: Calories: 123, Total Fat: 9 g, Protein: 2 g, Carbohydrate: 10 g, Cholesterol: 15 mg, Sodium: 56 mg, Dietary Fiber: 1 g Dietary Exchanges: ½ Bread, 2 Fat

Honey Ginger Snaps

2 cups all-purpose flour
1 tablespoon ground ginger
2 teaspoons baking soda
⅛ teaspoon salt
⅛ teaspoon ground cloves
½ cup vegetable shortening

¼ cup butter, softened
1½ cups sugar, divided
¼ cup honey
1 egg
1 teaspoon vanilla

PREHEAT oven to 350°F. Grease cookie sheets. Combine flour, ginger, baking soda, salt and cloves in medium bowl.

BEAT shortening and butter in large bowl with electric mixer at medium speed until smooth. Gradually beat in 1 cup sugar until blended; increase speed to high and beat until light and fluffy. Beat in honey, egg and vanilla until fluffy. Gradually stir in flour mixture until blended.

SHAPE mixture into 1-inch balls. Place remaining ½ cup sugar in shallow bowl; roll balls in sugar to coat. Place 2 inches apart on prepared cookie sheets.

BAKE 10 minutes or until golden brown. Let cookies stand on cookie sheets 5 minutes; transfer to wire racks to cool completely. Store in airtight container up to 1 week.   *Makes 42 cookies*

Nutrients per Serving: Calories: 90, Total Fat: 4 g, Protein: 1 g, Carbohydrate: 13 g, Cholesterol: 8 mg, Sodium: 75 mg, Dietary Fiber: trace Dietary Exchanges: 1 Bread, ½ Fat

Cook's Nook

For easy cleanup, coat your measuring cup with nonstick cooking spray before measuring out the honey (or any other sticky liquids). The honey will slide right out!

Double-Dipped Chocolate Peanut Butter Cookies

1¼ cups all-purpose flour
½ teaspoon baking powder
½ teaspoon baking soda
½ teaspoon salt
½ cup butter or margarine, softened
   Granulated sugar
½ cup packed light brown sugar
½ cup creamy or chunky peanut butter

1 egg
1 teaspoon vanilla
1½ cups semisweet chocolate chips
3 teaspoons shortening, divided
1½ cups milk chocolate chips

PREHEAT oven to 350°F. Combine flour, baking powder, baking soda and salt in small bowl.

BEAT butter, ½ cup granulated sugar and brown sugar in large bowl with electric mixer at medium speed until light and fluffy. Beat in peanut butter, egg and vanilla. Gradually stir in flour mixture until blended.

SHAPE heaping tablespoonfuls of dough into 1½-inch balls. Place balls 2 inches apart on *ungreased* cookie sheets. (If dough is too soft, refrigerate 30 minutes.)

DIP table fork into granulated sugar; press criss-cross fashion onto each ball, flattening to ½-inch thickness.

BAKE 12 minutes or until set. Let cookies stand on cookie sheets 2 minutes; transfer to wire racks to cool completely.

MELT semisweet chocolate chips and 1½ teaspoons shortening in heavy small saucepan over low heat. Dip one end of each cookie in mixture; place on waxed paper. Let stand until chocolate is set, about 30 minutes. Repeat with milk chocolate chips and remaining 1½ teaspoons shortening, dipping opposite ends of cookies. Store cookies between sheets of waxed paper in cool place or freeze up to 3 months.   *Makes about 24 (3-inch) cookies*

Nutrients per Serving: Calories: 236, Total Fat: 13 g, Protein: 4 g, Carbohydrate: 29 g, Cholesterol: 21 mg, Sodium: 155 mg, Dietary Fiber: 1 g Dietary Exchanges: 2 Bread, 2 Fat

Holiday Sugar Cookies

1 cup butter or margarine,
   softened
¾ cup sugar
1 egg
2 cups all-purpose flour
1 teaspoon baking powder
¼ teaspoon salt

¼ teaspoon ground
   cinnamon
Colored sprinkles,
   candies or colored
   sugar, for decorating
   (optional)

BEAT butter and sugar in large bowl with electric mixer until creamy. Add egg; beat until fluffy.

STIR in flour, baking powder, salt and cinnamon until well blended. Form dough into a ball; wrap in plastic wrap and flatten. Refrigerate about 2 hours or until firm.

PREHEAT oven to 350°F. Roll out dough, a small portion at a time, to ¼-inch thickness on lightly floured surface with lightly floured rolling pin. (Keep remaining dough wrapped in refrigerator.)

CUT out cookies with 3-inch cookie cutter. Decorate with sprinkles, candies or colored sugar, if desired. Transfer to *ungreased* cookie sheets.

BAKE 7 to 9 minutes until edges are lightly browned. Let cookies stand on cookie sheets 1 minute; transfer to wire racks to cool completely. Store in airtight container.   *Makes about 36 cookies*

Nutrients per Serving: Calories: 88, Total Fat: 5 g, Protein: 1 g,
Carbohydrate: 10 g, Cholesterol: 20 mg, Sodium: 77 mg, Dietary Fiber: trace
Dietary Exchanges: ½ Bread, 1 Fat

Raspberry Pecan Thumbprints

2 cups all-purpose flour
1 cup pecan pieces, finely
    chopped, divided
½ teaspoon ground
    cinnamon
¼ teaspoon ground allspice
⅛ teaspoon salt

1 cup butter, softened
½ cup packed light brown
    sugar
2 teaspoons vanilla
⅓ cup seedless raspberry
    jam

PREHEAT oven to 350°F. Combine flour, ½ cup pecans, cinnamon, allspice and salt in medium bowl.

BEAT butter in large bowl with electric mixer at medium speed until smooth. Gradually beat in sugar; increase speed to high and beat until light and fluffy. Beat in vanilla until blended. Beat in flour mixture at low speed just until blended.

FORM dough into 1-inch balls; flatten slightly and place on *ungreased* cookie sheets. Press down with thumb in center of each ball to form indentation. Pinch together any cracks in dough.

FILL each indentation with scant ½ teaspoon jam. Sprinkle filled cookies with remaining ½ cup pecans.

BAKE 14 minutes or until just set. Let cookies stand on cookie sheets 5 minutes; transfer to wire racks to cool completely. Store in airtight container at room temperature. Cookies are best day after baking.   *Makes 36 cookies*

Nutrients per Serving: Calories: 114, Total Fat: 8 g, Protein: 1 g,
Carbohydrate: 11 g, Cholesterol: 15 mg, Sodium: 17 mg, Dietary Fiber: 1 g
Dietary Exchanges: 1 Bread, 1 Fat

Molded Scotch Shortbread

1½ cups all-purpose flour　　**⅓ cup sugar**
　¼ teaspoon salt　　　　　　**1 egg**
　¾ cup butter, softened

PREHEAT oven to temperature recommended by shortbread mold manufacturer. Combine flour and salt in medium bowl.

BEAT butter and sugar in large bowl with electric mixer at medium speed until light and fluffy. Beat in egg. Gradually add flour mixture. Beat at low speed until well blended.

SPRAY 10-inch ceramic shortbread mold with nonstick cooking spray. Press dough firmly into mold. Bake, cool and remove from mold according to manufacturer's directions.

If mold is not available, preheat oven to 350°F. **SHAPE** tablespoonfuls of dough into 1-inch balls. Place 2 inches apart on *ungreased* cookie sheets; press with fork to flatten. Bake 18 to 20 minutes or until edges are lightly browned. Let cookies stand on cookie sheets 2 minutes; transfer to wire racks to cool completely. Store tightly covered at room temperature or freeze up to 3 months.

Makes 1 shortbread mold or 24 cookies

Nutrients per Serving: *Calories: 92, Total Fat: 6 g, Protein: 1 g, Carbohydrate: 9 g, Cholesterol: 24 mg, Sodium: 83 mg, Dietary Fiber: trace*
Dietary Exchanges: ½ Bread, 1 Fat

Butter can be stored in the refrigerator up to 1 month. Be sure to wrap it airtight, as butter readily absorbs flavors and odors from other items in the refrigerator.

Cocoa Crinkle Sandwiches

1¾ cups all-purpose flour
½ cup unsweetened cocoa
1 teaspoon baking soda
¼ teaspoon salt
½ cup butter
1¾ cups sugar, divided
2 eggs

2 teaspoons vanilla
1 can (16 ounces)
   chocolate or favorite
   flavor frosting
½ cup crushed candy
   canes* (optional)

COMBINE flour, cocoa, baking soda and salt in medium bowl.

MELT butter in large saucepan over medium heat; cool slightly. Add 1¼ cups sugar; whisk until smooth. Whisk in eggs, 1 at a time, until blended. Stir in vanilla until smooth. Stir in flour mixture just until combined. Wrap dough in plastic wrap; refrigerate 2 hours.

PREHEAT oven to 350°F. Grease cookie sheets. Shape dough into 1-inch balls. Place remaining ½ cup sugar in shallow bowl; roll balls in sugar. Place 1½ inches apart on cookie sheets.

BAKE 12 minutes or until cookies feel set to the touch. Let cookies stand on cookie sheets 5 minutes; transfer to wire racks to cool completely.

STIR frosting until soft and smooth. Place crushed candy canes on piece of waxed paper. Spread about 2 teaspoons frosting over flat side of one cookie. Place second cookie, flat side down, over frosting, pressing down to allow frosting to squeeze out slightly between cookies. Press exposed frosting into crushed candy canes. Repeat with remaining cookies. Store in airtight container.

    Makes about 20 sandwich cookies (about 40 unfilled cookies)

*To crush candy canes, place candy in sealed heavy-duty plastic food storage bag. Break into pieces with heavy object (such as meat mallet or can of vegetables); crush pieces with rolling pin.

Nutrients per Serving: *Calories: 251, Total Fat: 9 g, Protein: 2 g, Carbohydrate: 42 g, Cholesterol: 34 mg, Sodium: 186 mg, Dietary Fiber: trace Dietary Exchanges: 2½ Bread, 1½ Fat*

Pfeffernüsse

3½ cups all-purpose flour
2 teaspoons baking powder
1½ teaspoons ground cinnamon
1 teaspoon ground ginger
½ teaspoon baking soda
½ teaspoon salt
½ teaspoon ground cloves
½ teaspoon ground cardamom

¼ teaspoon freshly ground black pepper
1 cup butter, softened
1 cup granulated sugar
¼ cup dark molasses
1 egg
Powdered sugar

COMBINE flour, baking powder, cinnamon, ginger, baking soda, salt, cloves, cardamom and pepper in large bowl.

BEAT butter and granulated sugar in large bowl with electric mixer at medium speed until light and fluffy. Beat in molasses and egg. Gradually add flour mixture. Beat at low speed until dough forms. Shape dough into disk; wrap in plastic wrap and refrigerate until firm, 30 minutes or up to 3 days.

PREHEAT oven to 350°F. Grease cookie sheets. Roll dough into 1-inch balls. Place 2 inches apart on prepared cookie sheets.

BAKE 12 to 14 minutes or until golden brown. Transfer cookies to wire racks; dust with sifted powdered sugar. Cool completely. Store tightly covered at room temperature or freeze up to 3 months.

Makes about 60 cookies

Nutrients per Serving: Calories: 71, Fat: 3 g, Protein: 1 g, Carbohydrate: 10 g, Cholesterol: 12 mg, Sodium: 73 mg, Dietary Fiber: trace
Dietary Exchanges: ½ Bread, ½ Fat

Chocolate-Dipped Orange Logs

3¼ cups all-purpose flour
⅛ teaspoon salt
1 cup butter, softened
1 cup sugar
2 eggs
1½ teaspoons grated orange peel

1 teaspoon vanilla
1 package (12 ounces) semisweet chocolate chips
1½ cups pecan pieces, finely chopped

COMBINE flour and salt in medium bowl. Beat butter in large bowl with electric mixer at medium speed until smooth. Gradually beat in sugar; increase speed to high and beat until light and fluffy. Beat in eggs, 1 at a time, blending well after each addition. Beat in orange peel and vanilla until blended. Gradually stir in flour mixture until blended. (Dough will be crumbly.)

GATHER dough together and press gently to form a ball. Flatten into disk; wrap in plastic wrap and refrigerate 2 hours or until firm. (Dough can be prepared one day in advance and refrigerated overnight.)

PREHEAT oven to 350°F. Shape dough into 1-inch balls. Roll balls on flat surface with fingertips to form 3-inch logs about ½ inch thick. Place logs 1 inch apart on *ungreased* cookie sheets.

BAKE 14 minutes or until bottoms of cookies are golden brown. (Cookies will feel soft and look white on top; they will become crisp when cool.) Transfer to wire racks to cool completely.

For coating: **MELT** chocolate chips in medium heavy saucepan over low heat. Place chopped pecans on sheet of waxed paper. Dip one end of each cookie in chocolate, shaking off excess. Roll chocolate-covered ends with pecans. Place on waxed paper-lined cookie sheets and let stand until chocolate is set, or refrigerate about 5 minutes to set chocolate. Store in airtight container.   *Makes about 36 cookies*

Nutrients per Serving: Calories: 162, Total Fat: 10 g, Protein: 2 g, Carbohydrate: 8 g, Cholesterol: 23 mg, Sodium: 17 mg, Dietary Fiber: 1 g Dietary Exchanges: 1 Bread, 2 Fat

Gingerbread People

2¼ cups all-purpose flour
 2 teaspoons ground
    cinnamon
 2 teaspoons ground ginger
 1 teaspoon baking powder
½ teaspoon salt
¼ teaspoon ground cloves
¼ teaspoon ground nutmeg
¾ cup butter, softened

½ cup packed light brown
    sugar
½ cup dark molasses
 1 egg
    Prepared icing or gel-type
    tube frosting (optional)
    Candies and other
    decorations (optional)

COMBINE flour, cinnamon, ginger, baking powder, salt, cloves and nutmeg in large bowl.

BEAT butter and sugar in large bowl with electric mixer at medium speed until light and fluffy. Beat in molasses and egg. Gradually add flour mixture; beat at low speed until well blended. Shape dough into 3 disks. Wrap well in plastic wrap; refrigerate 1 hour or until firm.

PREHEAT oven to 350°F. Working with 1 disk at a time, place on lightly floured surface. Roll out dough with lightly floured rolling pin to ³⁄₁₆-inch thickness. Cut out gingerbread people with floured 5-inch cookie cutters; place on *ungreased* cookie sheets. Press dough trimmings together gently; reroll and cut out more cookies.

BAKE about 12 minutes or until edges are golden brown. Let cookies stand on cookie sheets 1 minute; transfer to wire racks to cool completely.

PIPE icing decoratively onto cooled cookies and decorate with candies, if desired. Let stand at room temperature 20 minutes or until set. Store tightly covered at room temperature or freeze up to 3 months. *Makes about 16 large cookies*

Nutrients per Serving: Calories: 193, Total Fat: 9 g, Protein: 2 g, Carbohydrate: 26 g, Cholesterol: 36 mg, Sodium: 191 mg, Dietary Fiber: trace
Dietary Exchanges: 2 Bread, 1½ Fat

Mexican Wedding Cookies

1 cup pecan pieces or halves

1 cup butter, softened

2 cups powdered sugar, divided

2 cups all-purpose flour, divided

2 teaspoons vanilla

⅛ teaspoon salt

PLACE pecans in food processor. Process using on/off pulses until pecans are ground, but not pasty.

BEAT butter and ½ cup powdered sugar in large bowl with electric mixer at medium speed until light and fluffy. Gradually add 1 cup flour, vanilla and salt. Beat at low speed until well blended. Stir in remaining 1 cup flour and ground pecans with spoon.

SHAPE dough into a ball; wrap in plastic wrap and refrigerate 1 hour or until firm.

PREHEAT oven to 350°F. Shape tablespoons of dough into 1-inch balls. Place 1 inch apart on *ungreased* cookie sheets.

BAKE 12 to 15 minutes or until pale golden brown. Let cookies stand on cookie sheets 2 minutes.

Meanwhile, **PLACE** 1 cup powdered sugar in 13×9-inch glass dish. Transfer hot cookies to powdered sugar. Roll cookies in powdered sugar, coating well. Let cookies cool in sugar.

SIFT remaining ½ cup powdered sugar over sugar-coated cookies before serving. Store tightly covered at room temperature or freeze up to 1 month. *Makes about 48 cookies*

Nutrients per Serving: *Calories: 90, Fat: 6 g, Protein: 1 g, Carbohydrate: 9 g, Cholesterol: 11 mg, Sodium: 12 mg, Dietary Fiber: trace*
Dietary Exchanges: ½ Bread, 1 Fat

Peanut Butter Chocolate Stars

1 cup peanut butter
1 cup packed light brown
   sugar
1 egg

48 milk chocolate candy
   stars or other solid milk
   chocolate candy

PREHEAT oven to 350°F. Line cookie sheets with parchment paper or leave ungreased.

COMBINE peanut butter, sugar and egg in medium bowl until blended and smooth.

SHAPE dough into 48 balls about 1½ inches in diameter. Place 2 inches apart on cookie sheets. Press one chocolate star on top of each cookie.

BAKE 10 to 12 minutes or until set. Transfer to wire racks to cool completely.

Makes 48 cookies

Nutrients per Serving: *Calories: 62, Total Fat: 3 g, Protein: 2 g, Carbohydrate: 7 g, Cholesterol: 5 mg, Sodium: 30 mg, Dietary Fiber: trace*
Dietary Exchanges: ½ Bread, ½ Fat

Cook's Nook

You can soften brown sugar in your microwave oven in no time. Simply place it in a covered dish and heat on HIGH for 30 to 60 seconds. (Watch the sugar to be sure it doesn't begin to melt; repeat the heating if necessary.)

Refrigerator Cookies

Choco-Coco Pecan Crisps

1 cup packed light brown
  sugar
½ cup butter or margarine,
  softened
1 egg
1 teaspoon vanilla

1½ cups all-purpose flour
1 cup chopped pecans
⅓ cup unsweetened cocoa
½ teaspoon baking soda
1 cup flaked coconut

BEAT sugar and butter in large bowl with electric mixer until blended. Beat in egg and vanilla.

COMBINE flour, pecans, cocoa and baking soda in small bowl. Add to butter mixture, stirring until stiff dough forms.

SPRINKLE coconut on work surface. Divide dough into 4 pieces. Shape each piece into log about 1½ inches in diameter; roll in coconut until thickly coated. Wrap in plastic wrap; refrigerate until firm, at least 1 hour or up to 2 weeks. (Or freeze up to 6 weeks.)

PREHEAT oven to 350°F. Line cookie sheets with parchment paper or leave ungreased. Cut logs into ⅛-inch-thick slices; place 2 inches apart on prepared cookie sheets.

BAKE 10 to 13 minutes or until firm and lightly browned. Transfer to wire racks to cool.   *Makes about 72 cookies*

Nutrients per Serving: Calories: 49, Total Fat: 3 g, Protein: 1 g, Carbohydrate: 6 g, Cholesterol: 6 mg, Sodium: 24 mg, Dietary Fiber: trace
Dietary Exchanges: ½ Bread, ½ Fat

Fruitcake Slices

1 cup butter or margarine, softened
1 cup powdered sugar
1 egg
1 teaspoon vanilla extract
1½ cups coarsely chopped candied fruit (fruitcake mix)

½ cup coarsely chopped walnuts
2½ cups all-purpose flour, divided
¾ to 1 cup flaked coconut
Maraschino cherry halves (optional)

BEAT butter in large bowl with electric mixer at medium speed until smooth. Add powdered sugar; beat until well blended. Add egg and vanilla; beat until well blended.

COMBINE candied fruit and walnuts in medium bowl. Stir ¼ cup flour into fruit mixture. Add remaining 2¼ cups flour to butter mixture; beat at low speed until blended. Stir in fruit mixture with spoon.

SHAPE dough into 2 logs, each about 5½ inches long and 2 inches in diameter. Spread coconut evenly on sheet of waxed paper. Roll logs in coconut, coating evenly. Wrap each log in plastic wrap. Refrigerate 2 to 3 hours or overnight, or freeze up to 1 month. (Let frozen logs stand at room temperature about 10 minutes before slicing and baking.)

PREHEAT oven to 350°F. Grease cookie sheets. Cut logs into ¼-inch-thick slices; place 1 inch apart on cookie sheets.

BAKE 13 to 15 minutes or until edges are golden brown. Transfer to wire racks to cool. Decorate with cherry halves, if desired. Store in airtight container.   *Makes about 48 cookies*

Nutrients per Serving: Calories: 67, Total Fat: 2 g, Protein: 1 g, Carbohydrate: 12 g, Cholesterol: 5 mg, Sodium: 13 mg, Dietary Fiber: trace Dietary Exchanges: ½ Bread

Spiced Wafers

½ cup butter or margarine,
　　softened
1 cup sugar
1 egg
2 tablespoons milk
1 teaspoon vanilla
1¾ cups all-purpose flour

2 teaspoon baking powder
1 teaspoon ground
　　cinnamon
½ teaspoon ground nutmeg
¼ teaspoon ground cloves
　Red colored sugar or red
　　hot candies (optional)

BEAT butter in large bowl with electric mixer at medium speed until smooth. Add sugar; beat until well blended. Add egg, milk and vanilla; beat until well blended.

COMBINE flour, baking powder, cinnamon, nutmeg and cloves in medium bowl. Gradually add flour mixture to butter mixture at low speed. Blend well after each addition.

SHAPE dough into 2 logs, each about 6 inches long and 2 inches in diameter. Wrap each log in plastic wrap. Refrigerate 2 to 3 hours or overnight.

PREHEAT oven to 350°F. Grease cookie sheets. Cut logs into ¼-inch-thick slices; sprinkle with colored sugar or candies, if desired. (Or leave plain and decorate with icing later.) Place at least 2 inches apart on cookie sheets.

BAKE 11 to 13 minutes or until edges are light brown. Transfer to wire racks to cool. Store in airtight container.

Makes about 48 cookies

Nutrients per Serving: Calories: 52, Total Fat: 2 g, Protein: 1 g, Carbohydrate: 8 g, Cholesterol: 10 mg, Sodium: 35 mg, Dietary Fiber: trace
Dietary Exchanges: ½ Bread, ½ Fat

Lip-Smacking Lemon Cookies

½ cup butter or margarine,
    softened
1 cup sugar
1 egg
2 tablespoons lemon juice
2 teaspoons grated lemon
    peel

2 cups all-purpose flour
1 teaspoon baking powder
⅛ teaspoon salt
    Dash ground nutmeg
    Yellow colored sugar
    (optional)

BEAT butter in large bowl with electric mixer at medium speed until smooth. Add sugar; beat until well blended. Add egg, lemon juice and peel; beat until well blended.

COMBINE flour, baking powder, salt and nutmeg in medium bowl. Gradually add flour mixture to butter mixture at low speed, blending well after each addition.

SHAPE dough into 2 logs, each about 6½ inches long and 1½ inches in diameter. Roll logs in colored sugar, if desired. Wrap each log in plastic wrap. Refrigerate 2 to 3 hours or up to 3 days.

PREHEAT oven to 350°F. Grease cookie sheets. Cut logs into ¼-inch-thick slices; place 1 inch apart on cookie sheets.

BAKE about 15 minutes or until edges are light brown. Transfer to wire rack to cool. Store in airtight container.

Makes about 48 cookies

Nutrients per Serving: Calories: 54, Total Fat: 2 g, Protein: 1 g, Carbohydrate: 8 g, Cholesterol: 10 mg, Sodium: 33 mg, Dietary Fiber: trace
Dietary Exchanges: ½ Bread, ½ Fat

Cappuccino Cookies

1 cup butter or margarine, softened
2 cups firmly packed brown sugar
2 tablespoons milk
2 tablespoons instant coffee granules
2 eggs
1 teaspoon rum extract

½ teaspoon vanilla
4 cups all-purpose flour
1 teaspoon baking powder
½ teaspoon ground nutmeg
¼ teaspoon salt
Chocolate sprinkles or melted chocolate (optional)

BEAT butter in large bowl with electric mixer at medium speed until smooth. Add sugar; beat until well blended.

HEAT milk in small saucepan over low heat; add coffee granules, stirring to dissolve. Add milk mixture, eggs, rum extract and vanilla to butter mixture. Beat at medium speed until well blended.

COMBINE flour, baking powder, nutmeg and salt in large bowl. Gradually add flour mixture to butter mixture, beating at low speed after each addition until blended.

SHAPE dough into 2 logs, about 8 inches long and 2 inches in diameter. (Dough will be soft; sprinkle lightly with flour if too sticky to handle.)

ROLL logs in chocolate sprinkles, if desired, coating evenly (⅓ cup sprinkles per roll). Or, leave rolls plain and dip cookies in melted chocolate after baking. Wrap each log in plastic wrap; refrigerate overnight.

PREHEAT oven to 350°F. Grease cookie sheets. Cut rolls into ¼-inch-thick slices; place 1 inch apart on cookie sheets. (Keep unbaked rolls and sliced cookies chilled until ready to bake.)

BAKE 10 to 12 minutes or until golden brown. Transfer to wire racks to cool. Dip plain cookies in melted semisweet or white chocolate, if desired.* Store in airtight container.   *Makes about 60 cookies*

*To dip 24 cookies, melt 1 cup chocolate chips in small saucepan over very low heat until smooth.

Nutrients per Serving: *Calories: 88, Total Fat: 3 g, Protein: 1 g, Carbohydrate: 14 g, Cholesterol: 15 mg, Sodium: 51 mg, Dietary Fiber: trace Dietary Exchanges: 1 Bread, ½ Fat*

Allspice: a mildly pungent and aromatic spice, so named because its flavor suggests a combination of cinnamon, cloves and nutmeg. Allspice is available in whole and ground forms and should be stored in a cool, dark place.

Cardamom: an aromatic spice with a pungent aroma and sweet, spicy flavor. Cardamom is available in whole pod, seed and ground forms and should be stored in a cool, dark place.

Cornstarch: a smooth powder made from corn. Cornstarch is most often used as a thickening agent, but is also used in combination with flour in some cookie and cake recipes to create a more delicate texture.

Corn Syrup: a thick, sweet syrup made from processing cornstarch. Both dark and light corn syrups are available; dark syrup has a stronger flavor and darker color than light syrup.

Cream of Tartar: a fine white powder often added to egg whites before beating to improve their stability and volume. Cream of tartar can be found in small jars where spices and baking ingredients are sold.

Fold in: to incorporate a light mixture (usually beaten egg whites or whipped cream) into a heavier mixture without deflating the lighter mixture. Folding is best done with a spatula and brief turning motions, without beating or stirring.

Macadamia Nut: a small, round nut with a sweet, buttery flavor, crisp texture and light color. Macadamia nuts are generally shelled and roasted before they are packaged; they can be found in tins and jars at the supermarket.

Molasses: a sweet, sticky syrup made from the process of refining sugar. Dark molasses is thicker, darker in color and not as sweet as light molasses.

Oats: fine-, medium- or coarse-textured cereal ground from hulled oats. Old-fashioned and quick-cooking oats can usually be interchanged unless the recipe directs otherwise.

Sweetened Condensed Milk: a mixture of milk and sugar heated until about half of the liquid evaporates. Sweetened condensed milk is available in cans and should not be confused with evaporated milk, which has no sugar added.

Sugar, Brown: a soft-textured mixture of granulated sugar and molasses. Brown sugar is commonly available in light and dark varieties, with dark brown sugar having a stronger flavor and darker color than light brown sugar. Both are often sold in—and shouid be stored in—plastic bags, which help the sugar retain its moisture and keep it soft.

Sugar, Powdered: granulated sugar that has been pulverized into a fine powder and mixed with a small amount of cornstarch to prevent clumping. Powdered sugar (or confectioners' sugar) is often used in icings and candies because it dissolves so easily. It is also used frequently as a decorative topping for many desserts.

METRIC CONVERSION CHART

VOLUME MEASUREMENTS (dry)

⅛ teaspoon = 0.5 mL

¼ teaspoon = 1 mL

½ teaspoon = 2 mL

¾ teaspoon = 4 mL

1 teaspoon = 5 mL

1 tablespoon = 15 mL

2 tablespoons = 30 mL

¼ cup = 60 mL

⅓ cup = 75 mL

½ cup = 125 mL

⅔ cup = 150 mL

¾ cup = 175 mL

1 cup = 250 mL

2 cups = 1 pint = 500 mL

3 cups = 750 mL

4 cups = 1 quart = 1 L

VOLUME MEASUREMENTS (fluid)

1 fluid ounce (2 tablespoons) = 30 mL

4 fluid ounces (½ cup) = 125 mL

8 fluid ounces (1 cup) = 250 mL

12 fluid ounces (1½ cups) = 375 mL

16 fluid ounces (2 cups) = 500 mL

WEIGHTS (mass)

½ ounce = 15 g

1 ounce = 30 g

3 ounces = 90 g

4 ounces = 120 g

8 ounces = 225 g

10 ounces = 285 g

12 ounces = 360 g

16 ounces = 1 pound = 450 g

DIMENSIONS

1/16 inch = 2 mm

⅛ inch = 3 mm

¼ inch = 6 mm

½ inch = 1.5 cm

¾ inch = 2 cm

1 inch = 2.5 cm

OVEN TEMPERATURES

250°F = 120°C

275°F = 140°C

300°F = 150°C

325°F = 160°C

350°F = 180°C

375°F = 190°C

400°F = 200°C

425°F = 220°C

450°F = 230°C

BAKING PAN SIZES

Utensil	Size in Inches/ Quarts	Metric Volume	Size in Centimeters
Baking or Cake Pan (square or rectangular)	8 × 8 × 2	2 L	20 × 20 × 5
	9 × 9 × 2	2.5 L	23 × 23 × 5
	12 × 8 × 2	3 L	30 × 20 × 5
	13 × 9 × 2	3.5 L	33 × 23 × 5
Loaf Pan	8 × 4 × 3	1.5 L	20 × 10 × 7
	9 × 5 × 3	2 L	23 × 13 × 7
Round Layer Cake Pan	8 × 1½	1.2 L	20 × 4
	9 × 1½	1.5 L	23 × 4
Pie Plate	8 × 1¼	750 mL	20 × 3
	9 × 1¼	1 L	23 × 3
Baking Dish or Casserole	1 quart	1 L	—
	1½ quart	1.5 L	—
	2 quart	2 L	—